# LOVE YOU
## even tho'...

Written by Herbert I. Kavet

*To Jack "85"*
*When you get*
*bored, please*
*read!*
*I marked the*
*ones that*
*suit you!*
*→*

AN **Ivory Tower** BOOK
**Contemporary Books, Inc.**
**Chicago**

Published by Contemporary Books, Inc.
180 North Michigan Avenue, Chicago, Illinois 60601
Manufactured in the United States of America
International Standard Book Number: 0-8092-5341-0

# I Love You
## even tho'...

You wake up with the worst breath
I've ever smelled.

# I Love You even tho'...

People take their lives in their hands
when you drive.

You can't hold your liquor.

A gourmet cook you're not.

Your choice of gifts is sometimes queer.

Your choice in music is bizarre.

# I Love You
## even tho'...

Your pets add nothing to my life.

# I Love You even tho'...

You'll never win a prize for neatness.

Keeping a secret isn't one of your stronger points.

# I Love You even tho'...

You rarely remember my birthday
and never our anniversary.

# *I Love You even tho'...*

A spendthrift you'll never be.

# I Love You even tho'...

Your decorating skills could be the subject
of a Salvation Army study.

# I Love You even tho'...

A brilliant conversationalist you'll never be.

Your mathematical skills cannot be expanded
to include balancing the checkbook.

# I Love You even tho'...

Waiters snicker when you try to order wine.

# I Love You
## even tho'...

You can't resist a bargain.

# I Love You even tho'...

I need to make an appointment
to use the bathroom.

# I Love You even tho'...

You use every door handle and bedpost as a hanger.

# I Love You
## even tho'...

Your clothing coordination proves you **can**
screw up a designer collection.

You wear the rattiest underwear I've ever seen.

# *I Love You even tho'...*

Your relatives all need psychiatric help.

Saving money isn't exactly your forte.

# I Love You even tho'...

Your menu planning sometimes lacks imagination.

# I Love You even tho'...

Our vacations are always a compromise.

You're one of the phone company's biggest profit
centers.

Your politics are appalling.

Your idea of a good time sometimes
leaves me uninspired.

# I Love You even tho'...

You've gained a teenie bit of weight
since we first met.

# I Love You even tho'...

You pick your nose when stuck in traffic.

# I Love You even tho'...

Your friends are likely candidates for
institutionalization.

# I Love You
## even tho'...

You generate more laundry than a football squad.

# I Love You
## even tho'...

Your sense of timing never ceases to amaze me.

# I Love You even tho'...

An intellectual you'll never be mistaken for.

You tell the punch lines to my jokes.

# I Love You even tho'...

You hog all the closets.

# I Love You even tho'...

Your interest in sex is unceasing.

X

I'd rather share a bathroom with a chimpanzee.

# I Love You even tho'...

Your diets drive me crazy.

# I Love You even tho'...

Other people's bodies turn your head.

*Watch this!*

# *I Love You*
## *even tho'...*

We never agree on TV programs.

Somehow you seem to disappear when there are chores to be done.

I sometimes fail to appreciate your creativity.

# I Love You even tho'...

A romantic person you will never be.

Every evening!

You are the grouchiest person in the morning.

You make my drinks too strong.

You have no understanding of etiquette.

# I Love You even tho'...

You never quite know how to welcome me home.

You sometimes fail to notice when I'm feeling low.

I could probably live without your hobbies.

# I Love You even tho'...

My desserts are never my own.

# I Love You
## even tho'...

You always clog the drains with hair.

# I Love You even tho'...

Your choice of ties is appalling.

# I Love You even tho'...

You never seem to realize when I need to be alone.

You never seem to realize when I really need a hug.

# I Love You even tho'...

Your mother never taught you to share.

*Especially this one!*

*X.*

I Love You even tho'...

Mid-town Mall

It sometimes takes you a little longer
to make up your mind.

I Love You even tho'...

You don't always respect other people's property.

# I Love You even tho'...

You never turn the lights out.

# I Love You
## even tho'...

You sometimes leave things for the last minute.

# I Love You even tho'...

Your sense of direction is a joke.

You never learned to live within our means.

I Love You even tho'...

You hog all the best parts of the newspaper.

# I Love You
## even tho'...

You're sometimes a little impatient when teaching.

# I Love You
## even tho'...

You beat me at some of my favorite sports.

# I Love You even tho'...

You're forever borrowing my stuff.

# I Love You
## even tho'...

Our backgrounds are incredibly different.

XXX

You're always late.

# *I Love You even tho'...*

It takes you forever to understand
simple mechanical things.

# I Love You even tho'...

The neighbors all complain.

# I Love You even tho'...

Your idea of necessities makes me cry.

You've been known to fudge your tax returns.

# I Love You even tho'...

Your dependability is sometimes questionable.

# I Love You even tho'...

We are never able to dance together.

# I Love You even tho'...

You always sing off-key.

# I Love You even tho'...

Your parents never taught you common courtesy.

# I Love You
## even tho'...

You have the coldest feet.

# I Love You
## even tho'...

You have no self-control.

# *I Love You even tho'...*

A cooperative person you are not.

# I Love You even tho'...

We never agree on bedtimes.

# I Love You even tho'...

My family thinks you came from another planet.

# *I Love You even tho'...*

You take the lousiest pictures.

# I Love You even tho'...

You never clean the refrigerator.

# I Love You even tho'...

You never listen to what I'm saying.

You are a storehouse of totally useless information.

You embarrass me at work.

# I Love You
## even tho'...

I'm still not exactly sure what you do at work.

# I Love You even tho'...

I'm the only person who can decipher
your handwriting.

# I Love You
## even tho'...

Your handy skills extend only to changing
light bulbs.

# I Love You even tho'...

You obtain all your news from the most dubious sources.

# I Love You even tho'...

Our weekends seldom are a source
of cerebral stimulation.

# I Love You even tho'...

We never agree on room temperature.

# I Love You even tho'...

The strangest things turn you on.

# I Love You
## even tho'...

I love you with and for all your quirks and foibles
and, after laughing at them all, you are still
the one who turns me on.

These other humorous titles are available at fine bookstores or by sending $3.95 each plus $1.00 per book to cover postage and handling to the address below.

Please send me:

| QUAN. | | TITLE |
|---|---|---|
| | **5352-6** | Skinny People Are Dull and Crunchy Like Carrots |
| | **5370-4** | A Coloring Book for Pregnant Mothers to Be |
| | **5367-4** | Games You Can't Lose |
| | **5358-5** | The Trite Report |
| | **5357-7** | Happy Birthday Book |
| | **5356-9** | Adult Crossword Puzzles |
| | **5359-3** | Bridget's Workout Book |
| | **5360-7** | Picking Up Girls |
| | **5368-2** | Games for the John |
| | **5340-2** | Living in Sin |
| | **5341-0** | I Love You Even Tho' . . . |
| | **5342-9** | You Know You're Over 50 When . . . |
| | **5363-1** | You Know You're Over 40 When . . |
| | **5361-5** | Wimps |
| | **5354-2** | Sex Manual for People Over 30 |
| | **5353-4** | Small Busted Women Have Big Hearts |
| | **5369-0** | Games You Can Play with Your Pussy Cat (and Lots of Other Stuff Cat Owners Should Know) |
| | **5366-6** | Calories Don't Count If You Eat Standing Up |
| | **5365-8** | Do Diapers Give You Leprosy? What Every Parent Should Know About Bringing Up Babies |
| | **5355-0** | I'd Rather Be 40 Than Pregnant |
| | **5362-3** | Afterplay: How to Get Rid of Your Partner After Sex |

Send me _____ books at $3.95* each                    $_____

Illinois residents add 8% sales tax; California residents add 6% sales tax:    _____

Add $1.00 per book for shipping/handling                           _____

                                              **TOTAL $**_____

☐ Check or M.O. payable to Best Publications

Charge my   ☐ Visa   ☐ MasterCard

Acct. #_____ Exp. Date ____/____

X_____

Signature (required only if charging to Bankcard)

Name _____

Address_____

_____

City/State/Zip_____

*Prices subject to change without notice.

Best Publications, Department IT

180 N. Michigan Ave., Chicago, IL 60601                    BB 0784